CAREER-LIFE-DESIGN FOR YOUNG PEOPLE

GOODNESS

and

KINDNESS

A CURRENCY FOR SUCCESS

DR ADELINE TWIGGE

CONTENTS

ADELINE TWIGGE

PREFACE

SOCIETY URGENTLY NEEDS LARGE SCALE SYSTEMIC CHANGE

In today's pervasive elitist, narcissistic industrialized society, it is more important than ever to understand our interdependency on each other and with the environment. By developing an astute awareness of the relationships in our life-giving environment, we can counter the human-centred operating manual for life which comprises environmental-ecological, socioeconomic, and geopolitical issues.

THE MULTIPLIER EFFECT

Imagine an innovative engine – a youth collective of citizen and global leaders – that rapidly generates lots and lots of goodwill (solutions for local and global challenges) that penetrates the human landscape and change it for the better. Imagine mobilizing the vast untapped potential of novel and modern young leaders using their innovative ideas and contributions in a spirit of goodwill to promote social harmony directly and indirectly – a multiplier effect.

And in return, together with having personal purpose and meaning added to their own lives, they as youth would create a peaceful and affluent environment that exudes wellbeing on every level. In this way, the common good can and will be sustained and continuously expanded in service of fair and sustainable human development globally.

AIM OF THE E-BOOK

The aim of the e-book is to share a career-life-design perspective which can potentially serve as a way to encourage young people to design an ideal self (identity) that enables them to contribute to their own development and the development of a healthy and sustainable environment. As such, they become part of a potential resource of citizen and/or global leaders.

THEREFORE

By using a career-life-design narrative, young people are invited to become the authors of their own new stories (a new identity, a new self) wherein a sense of the good can be woven.

 Taylor, 1989, p. 197 declares: "In order to make minimal sense of our lives, in order to have an identity, we need an orientation to the good, and we see that this sense of the good has to be woven into my understanding of my life as an unfolding story."

In summary, the deduction can be made that:

> *"Magic in one's career-life happens where your deep*
> *gladness and the world's deep hunger meet."*

And as such, a positive and informed narrative can be converted into action.

FOREWORD

I met Dr. Adeline Twigge in 1999 when we were both newly qualified psychologists working at a remedial school in Germiston, South Africa. Since then, I have seen Dr. Twigge's love for the youth and her passion for working with young people, in particular emerging adults and millennials, grow and blossom into a Doctorate degree focussed on assisting young people with life path design, and subsequent to that into this informative eBook. Dr. Twigge has passionately dedicated her life to guiding youth (and also the not so youthful) towards transformation of their own lives as well as their life worlds with the goal of expanding the overall wellbeing for the individual, families, communities and the greater good of society.

There is a Chinese proverb that states:

If you are planning for a year, sow rice;

if you are planning for a decade, plant trees;

if you are planning for a lifetime, educate people.

Dr. Twigge is doing just this by educating young people and providing them with the skills to write their own narratives with the focus on their unique character strengths and 'Sparks'. This eBook also makes the important connection between young people being the authors of their own narratives and the impact of the individual on the society they live in. Each person's story defines the individual's life path which in turn impacts the narrative for communities and society as a whole, which then becomes the universal, collective narrative of our time. A whole generation of young people defining their individual futures by using their unique gifts and 'Sparks' – to further the common good and the wellbeing of all – will have this generation planning for a lifetime!

A quote by the Dalai Lama captures the essence of the tapestry of our own individual stories and personal purpose, woven into our communities and broader into our global society: "The true essence of humankind is kindness. There are other qualities which come from education or knowledge, but it is essential, if one wishes to be a genuine human being and impart satisfying meaning to one's existence, to have a good heart." We are all connected by our humanness, and how beautiful it will be if all our stories are connected by the golden thread of goodness and kindness.

In this eBook Dr. Twigge has given the youth a valuable perspective from where they can create their life stories. Life stories filled with their own individual 'sparks' and aimed at the improvement of the wellbeing of our global society and with the potential for a fulfilling, thriving collective and universal story.

Dr. Annelien Nieman
December 2019
Somerset West
South Africa

Dr. Annelien Nieman is an Educational Psychologist in private practice, as well as an Enneagram coach. Her focus is on holistic healing using Mindfulness and meditation.

GRATITUDE

I would like to share my sincere gratitude of growing up in a spiritual environment (household and religious) where good old values like "love thy neighbour as thyself" were and still are educated and lived.

Furthermore, I would love to acknowledge Professor Kobus Maree who has been my mentor in conducting my research on the value of career-life-design counselling for young people.

Lastly, I would like to acknowledge the team around the preparing and publishing of this e-book. This would be:

My son Arthur Twigge for coming up with the catchy title of this e-book;

The illustrator of the artwork in this e-book, namely Imile Wepener who really has the gift to condense a thousand words into one vibrant picture!

Dave Henderson with his wonderful MYeBOOK Self-Publishing Team whom assisted me in creating, polishing, publishing and marketing this e-book within an astonishing record-breaking time!

INTRODUCTION

1

Dear (more or less) 1.8 billion Young People,

Do you know that there have never been so many young people as right now? And do you know that likely, there will never again be such potential for wellbeing-for-all on our planet? And do you know that how you become involved in the futuristic story of mankind, will define the common future of all?

But let me firstly introduce you to the storyline in which all of you are going to play a heroic and leading role. I am sure we can all agree that we want our story to have a happy ending, and for our grandchildren and their grandchildren and future generations to also all live happily hereafter! For this kind of happy ending and happy hereafters, we need to exchange a few further insights, which will be open ended, of course. After all, it is our story and we can change and adapt it as we wish.

Taylor (1989, p. 197) writes the following: ... *in order to make minimal sense of our lives, in order to have an identity, we need an orientation to the good, and ... we see that this sense of the good has to be woven into my understanding of my life as an unfolding story*. A first basic principle would then be to realize that goodness and kindness will need to play a prominent role in the unfolding of our story.

The second basic principle is to realize you all have unique character strengths, interests, talents, capacities, and skills, which we will call *sparks*[1] (Scales, Benson & Roehlkepartain, 2010). A *spark* and an *opportunity* become potent together, and this fact emerges as our third simple principle: A *spark* needs an *opportunity* to become really *sparky!* A logic conclusion is that you and others whom all have an awareness of your own *sparks*, will need to choose *opportunities* (including the important actions of choosing and accomplishing a career) where you feel you can make a positive difference in your more immediate environment (locally, as a "civilian self/individual") and in the world (more globally, as a "cosmopolitan self/individual"), and then start firing!

And since our project is so huge, we will have to realize that we are all in it together – old and young, but the (too) old ones and the (too) young ones will all need YOUR help. And YOU are the ones with ages, let's say approximately from sixteen years old to those in their thirties, because you constitute our "globals". As the UN Millennium Project notes: "Ours (all our young people) is the first generation with the means to know the world as a whole and to improve global systems. This does not mean world government; it means world governance."

Let's describe our planet as one big organism and whoever gets together wherever and however, are the organs. And since part of the basis of a healthy body is the nervous system, all of you in your different and diverse groups will have to start to fire together – in modern language, it means you young people, as our favorite (and hopefully self-appointed!) global stewards of the earth, will have to network, network, network. Good thing you are all so good at that!

Figure 1: Young people attending the web of life.

Buechner (1993:119) positions a person's life journey neatly as an answer to a call, namely *The place God calls you to is the place where your deep gladness and the world's deep hunger meet*, whilst Savickas (2006, 2011b:13) adds power to this statement with his observation that something special (magic) happens if there is movement: *Magic happens when we move [forward]*. The value of the dynamics can thus be compiled in a nutshell by combining Buechner's (1993) and Savickas's (2006, 2011b:13) remarks: ***The magic happens where your deep gladness and the world's deep hunger meet.***

A line from Robert Frost's poem titled A Red, Red Rose confirms my own conviction that when man finds harmony between his own deep joy and the world's deep hunger, the result is a melodious product: *O my Luve is like a red, red rose. That's newly sprung in June; O my Luve is like the melody. That's sweetly played in tune.*

The invitation is then to allow yourself to become tuned in to the music of the greater whole and see how an awesome, magical power starts unfolding in your life! And moreover, if you invite others to do good together with you or if you support any other positive quest, the promise is: *When people come together to do what they love, something symphonic/magical happens!*

Let's do this together!

SO, WHAT TO DO?!

Parks (2011) remarks that people in ancient societies gathered together in great plazas and squares in cities and villages around the world which was called the "commons". She states furthermore that *people gathered on the commons for commerce and communication, play and protest, memorial and celebration, and worked out how they would live together over time* (Parks, 2011, p. 15).

As you will see, our story will be a suggestion on how a commons entrenched with goodness and kindness could look and feel. The picture you can sort of create in your mind is a circulatory system, consisting of loops of healthy interdependency between mindsets and activities of all sorts. The logistics of the commons we speak about here refers to either individuals' local or physical settings (where civilian selves/individuals can find solutions to local challenges) or a digital commons (where cosmopolitan selves/ individuals can find solutions to more global issues).

To achieve this, "vertical towers" or "isolated" perceptions and ideologies need to be toppled and re-structured into interconnectedly layered and stacked building blocks. But we need to understand that values will always differ from one community to the next, and as such, we will have to be lenient in finding common principles that could link a range of values held by different groups. In the foreword of renowned clinical psychologist and professor of psychology, Jordan Peterson's book "12 Rules of Life" (2018, p. xxii), Norman Doidge mentions that *For the ancients, the discovery that different people have different ideas about how, practically, to live, did not paralyze them; it deepened their understanding of humanity and led to some of the most satisfying conversations human beings ever had, about how life might be lived.*

In short, the proposal is a new model for human development and thus, a new mankind. Zogby (2008) summarizes it neatly as a *fundamental reorientation of character, away from wanton consumption and toward a new global citizenry in an age of limited resources* (Zogby quoted in Halal, 2013). In their compendium of character strengths and virtues and under the umbrella of Positive Psychology, Peterson and Seligman (2004) identified six universal virtues that are common across a broad sample of cultures, religions, and moral philosophers: wisdom, courage, humanity, justice, temperance, and transcendence. Furthermore, the authors (Peterson and Seligman) have extrapolated numerous character strengths that exemplify each of the six universal virtues[2] and delineated it further as the way we as human beings uniquely separate ourselves from animals and display our human essence.

Figure 2: We need a fundamental reorientation of character toward a new kind of citizenry

On the side-line, in a VIA Strengths (2015) YouTube video clip called "A character strengths revolution", Mayerson voiced a fear many people share about technology displacing jobs, but he counteracted it with the remark that ... *the skills needed most in the 21st Century – character strengths like curiosity, creativity, taking initiative, multi-disciplinary thinking, and empathy – happen to be skills that machines don't have; only humans have it.* He states optimistically that although we can hardly expect a perfect world, it could become a reasonably functioning global order: *As we attend to what is good in ourselves and in others, good things happen for us all. In other words, attending to what is good, creates greater goodness.*

As such, you are invited to take a free personality survey as to discover your character strengths with the "VIA Institute on Character" website. Niemiec (2013) has written an eight-session program which systematically boosts awareness and application of character strengths which can aid you in your quest to flourish and lead a more fulfilling life. In conjunction with these character strengths, Rashid and Anjum (2011) suggest 340 ways to practice and use the via character strengths as to develop oneself, but also to contribute to society.

In psychological terms, we aim for self-efficacy – the belief in our ability to achieve goals. High self-efficacy has been linked to self-regulation, resilience and accomplishment (Bandura, 1988).

Jordan Peterson underscores the fact that all of us need to adopt as much responsibility as possible for individual life, society, and the world. To his mind, it is the fundamental question of meaning and purpose of how we should live as human beings. Peterson's answer to this fundamental question is surprisingly simple: *You have a moral obligation or a responsibility to yourself and your loved ones to aim at the greatest good according to your conscience and best understanding, then to pursue it each day with discipline, integrity, and courage* (Wong, 2019).

Peterson, Higgins and Pihl (2019) designed a Self-Authoring Suite which is essentially a series of online exercises covering your past, present, and future. It asks you to write about, analyze, and decode significant experiences in your past, define your faults and strengths, and build a plan for the future.

In a now-famous appearance on JRE Clips (2017), "The Joe Rogan Experience", Peterson announced that, before you start improving the world, you have to start by "Clean up your room. That's a good start." One of Peterson's main theories is that cleaning your room is related to many other positive outcomes. Now, obviously, he doesn't mean *literally* cleaning your room. It's a metaphor for getting your own life in order first before you try to contribute to the greater good: *You start small. Your room is an externalization of your mind. To the degree that you are in your room, the room is you. Straighten up what you can straighten up and quit saying things that make you feel weak. And then you'll know what to do next* (Jordan Peterson Clip, 2017).

Thus, Peterson dares to paint responsibility in its raw nakedness. The alternative is unthinkable – it means living out the rest of one's life, as he states it: *in the living hell of unfulfilled promise, guilt, and regret* (Wong, 2019). This is a noble path which demands dedication, but it holds the promise of experiencing a meaningful and thus fulfilling life.

In summary, taking responsibility means to write your own glorious story which then becomes the blueprint of making wellbeing your own, as well as promoting it in others and the environment you are surrounded with. And as you can see, there are more than enough tools that can support you in planning and becoming your best future self. Now, let's look at your personal story and see what broad guidelines might support you in designing a career-life that offers wellbeing to yourself and to others. To accomplish this feat, we are going to consider career-life-design, which will be discussed in the next session.

CAREER-LIFE-DESIGN 3

Before we proceed with the design of your career-life, we need to distinguish between the three categories of career services, namely vocational guidance, career education and life design. Vocational guidance involves matching people to fitting positions and makes use of scores. The scores are obtained from the results of questionnaires and inventories with reference to, for instance, on an individual's interests, abilities and personality.

Career education refers to educational methods that support individuals and groups to develop specific knowledge and skills they need for a specific career path. Examples are hands-on training in occupational fields such as cosmetology, welding, commercial truck driving (and many more) or planning the how, what and where on a chosen academic field (for instance which college or university to attend).

Life design focusses on constructing a positive personal life and/ or career story which can be rewritten as needed. It allows an individual to step back and oversee the current story when new life conditions cause rapid adaptation. By means of critical self-reflection, a new ideal life is designed wherein a decision is made towards how to use one's work in a meaningful life. In this way life and career is seen as life-long designing (Savickas, 2011).

So, let's bite on our teeth and get the job done. Firstly, should you wish to design a life (which includes obtaining adequate vocational skills) to benefit yourself and others, you will need to understand the bigger picture – that all of us on planet Earth are connected and the actions of one has an influence on the other.

Thus, you should ask yourself where the world's deepest hunger is so that you might feed it with your spark(s) in a good, kind and ethical way, and apply the answer to this question when designing your own career-life.

For instance, in a Mindvalley Talk (2016) on YouTube called "An alternative model to success", Vishen Lakhiani suggests you ask the question: *What is your vision of paradise on Earth? What is that one thing that really captivates you that you would love to see more of in the world today?* Your answer to this question would be the "opportunity" that was mentioned in the introduction. Concurrently, you need to combine your personal spark with the opportunity you identified. And off you go!

Figure 3: Find your magic! — an opportunity that meets your spark

The quest then is to create a personal narrative that can inspire and empower you to pursue new, life-enhancing ways to live. And the real question is: how do you interweave a sense of the good – everlasting spiritual values and ideals – in your own career-life as an unfolding story?

4

There are two world views that seem important for designing a career-life which incorporates a contribution to the greater good. The one world view is a self-fulfilling (self-centered) world view and the other, a self-transcending one. Both are important as it contributes to seeing the bigger picture, as already mentioned, that we are all connected and the actions of the one has an influence on the other.

The first world view refers to someone who is inclined to develop her- or himself to become her or his "best self" or "ideal self" (a self-fulfilling worldview). The second world view refers to someone who applies her- or himself to the greater good – who considers others' needs as important as his or her own (a self-transcending worldview). The magic trick is to be able to balance the two.

Figure 4: A balanced oscillation between self-centeredness and "other"-centeredness

With reference to the self-fulfilling or self-centered world view, you are encouraged to develop your character strengths, talents, abilities, skills, interests, and passions. In a way, you are encouraged to become your "best self", which means becoming a person capable of managing yourself and providing for your own needs (see Attachment A, pages 25 to 31, which provides examples of dimensions and indicators of successful personal development).

With reference to the self-transcending world view, you are encouraged to identify and practice your unique spark and then apply it on your own or with others to some local or global opportunity that cries for a solution (see Attachment B, pages 33 to 38 for an insight into examples of major problems which threaten the sustainability of Planet Earth).

And when it comes to developing your "relational-moral self"[3] or "spiritual self", it has been found that participating in organized youth groups – consisting of friends, mentors, and youth leaders – that focus on aspects of wellbeing (individual wellbeing and societal wellbeing), work well (Schwartz, Bukowski & Aoki, 2006; Maree & Twigge, 2015). Another interesting aspect is that, with regards to work environments, Dik and Duffy (2009) found that young people with a spiritual approach or orientation (employees that have good values and strive to attain healthy relationships) seem to be more successful in finding and keeping a job or career.

As already mentioned, contexts that beg for "sparky interference" are the civilian and the cosmopolitan arena. With regards to your civilian self, be on the look-out for the many community-oriented projects in which you and other young people can become involved. As a cosmopolitan self, the web is the way to go! See if you can find co-creators with the same interests and passions that you have and grow your ideas together.

Now, everything comes together for a beautiful personal and (indirectly) global positive and meaningful narrative. Imagine this innovative engine – your tribe, in other words, all of you – that rapidly generates lots and lots of goodwill (solutions for local and global challenges) which penetrates the human landscape and change it for the better. And in return, together with having lovely personal purpose and meaning added to your own lives (you will start thriving), you would be creating a peaceful and affluent environment with wellbeing entrenched in it on all levels (in other words, a world which is also thriving) for yourselves and others. In this way, good and kind behavior as well as a better world can and will be sustained as well as continuously expanded – a currency for success. And that's our goal, isn't it?

*Figure 5: A positive and informed narrative
to be converted into action*

Furthermore, as the author of your own story, your tribe has the opportunity – and indirectly, sort of the responsibility – to play a vital role in the development of a new model of leadership, rooted in the humane. Let's see what it implies.

A NEW KIND OF GLOBAL LEADERSHIP

5

The world urgently requires relational-moral leaders who see the bigger picture, as we all are losing out because of the limited, outdated view of some leaders today – a disconnected, individualistic, and fragmentary perspective. Therefore, it is critical that a shift is made to a new kind of leadership. Such a leadership would comprise of individuals who have a deep sense of the interconnectedness of all, together with a drive for communal responsibility (see figure 5).

Figure 5 expresses the following: When you as a young person 1) accepts the notion of a balanced oscillation between your own needs and desires and the needs and desires of others, and furthermore, 2) combine your spark and meaningful activities within a spirit of goodwill, you become 3) a relational-moral self that becomes a citizen and/or global leader, 4) attending the web of life.

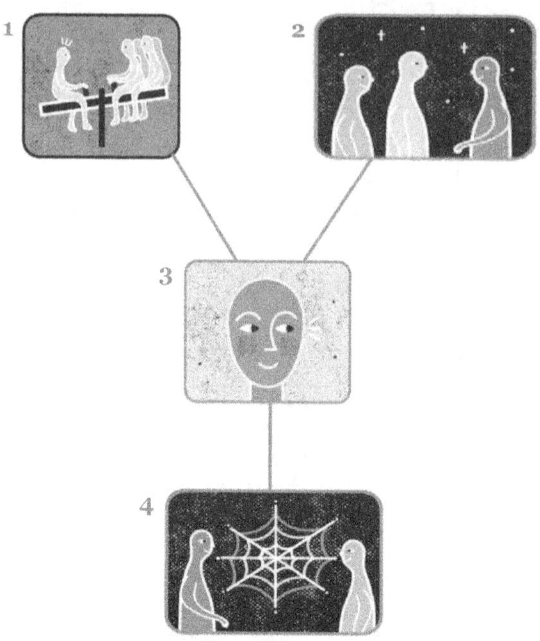

Figure 6: Become a relational-moral leader who sees the bigger picture by accommodating the needs of others and by matching your spark with an opportunity in the spirit of goodwill

An example of a values-based model of empowering youth to become (relational-moral) leaders, is Columba Leadership in South Africa – founded in 2009. It is a movement which motivates and equips large numbers of responsible young leaders to start being the change they want to see in their communities. The founder of Columba Leadership, Rob Taylor, declared the success of the model in the following statement: *To be driven by a desire to serve their own communities rather than just self- interest, is the key.* He adds wisely: *any society built on rights with no responsibility is in for a tough ride* (Taylor, 2016, p. 1).

In a Big Think (2018) YouTube video clip, Peterson combines responsibility and leadership. He cautions that before any young

leader starts with improving the world, he or she must firstly set their own house in order. Leaders, according to him, must be strongly rooted to the ethics or qualities that they want to inculcate in others. In addition, a leader's job isn't to motivate people; it's to tap into people's sense of purpose – in other words, to match a spark with an opportunity.

In conclusion, a good story starts with your core relation-moral self as the author of your own story, with the vision to contribute your spark – together with like-minded co-creators – to the greater story of society. It might play out in your career or as a passionate hobby while living life. That's why it is called career-life-design. In so doing, all of you become influential leaders that turn others on to also spread goodness and kindness, which can become our planet's currency for success. Therefore, true leaders unlock the potential for greatness in themselves, and in those they serve.

You are invited to join the revolution to fill the world with goodness. Find your spark, be open for opportunities, live your character strengths aloud, and encourage at least one other person into doing the same. Write your story; live your story. As Mayerson states unequivocally in the VIAStrengths (2015) video clip: *Our best is yet to come, its right in front of us, it's there to be had, thank you!*

DIMENSIONS AND INDICATORS OF SUCCESSFUL YOUNG ADULTHOOD

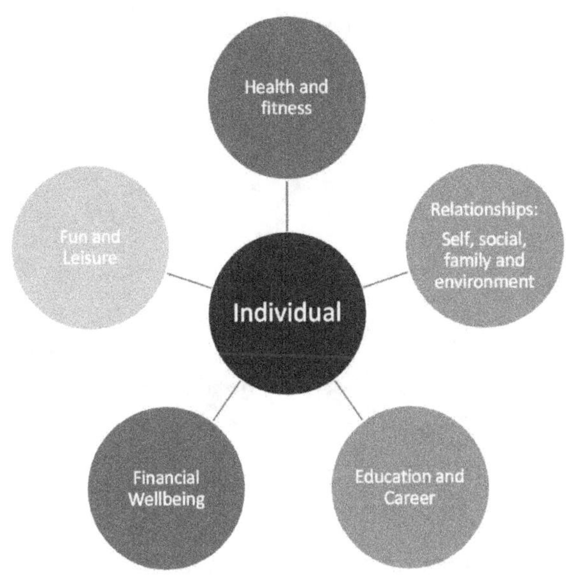

(Adapted from: Scales, Benson, Oesterle, Hill, Hawkins, David, Pashak & Travis, 2015)

1. HEALTH AND FITNESS

SUCCESSFUL YOUNG ADULTS:

Keep their bodies healthy and manage their body weight by following a nutritious and healthy diet, exercising regularly and getting enough and regular sleep.

Keep their bodies healthy by preventative health care (regular medical and dental check-ups), and protection against unplanned pregnancy and sexually transmitted diseases by practicing safe sex and always using condoms.

Honour their bodies by avoiding binge drinking, using tobacco, illegal drugs and abusing over the counter medication, and by seeking help for addiction when needed.

Engages in safe and responsible driving habits by respecting traffic rules, wearing seatbelts and not driving under the influence of drugs, alcohol and medication.

2. RELATIONSHIPS

Successful young adults value healthy relationships with self, others, community and the environment.

2.1 SELF

They have a positive and optimistic outlook and are accepting of themselves.

They seek personal development and growth in order to facilitate living a meaningful and purposeful life characterised by self-awareness and acceptance, emotional regulation and goal setting.

They acquire practical skills in order to pursue educational, occupational and relationship goals and to deal with challenges and disappointments.

They make independent and responsible decisions with regards to life choices (marriage, parenting, employment) and financial wellbeing. Financially they live within their means, pay bills on time and save.

They ask for guidance and assistance from parents, elders and qualified advisors when needed.

They develop and live with a sense of purpose which is meaningful to themselves and beneficial to others and the environment.

They are prosocial – they engage in healthy interpersonal relationships and interactions and develop skills to improve social interactions such as efficient communication and interpersonal conflict.

They take responsibly for themselves and their decisions, and the consequences of their decisions. They do not blame others or make excuses for their behaviour.

They focus on cultivating a mindful state of intentional open awareness to sensations, emotions, thoughts and perception. Mindfulness can increase positive emotion as well as emotional regulation and excellence in one's being. A mindful state can also reduce negative emotional states such as anxiety and depression, and unhealthy habitual and reactive coping skills.

2.2 HEALTHY FAMILY AND SOCIAL RELATIONSHIPS

They strive to establish and maintain meaningful personal and social relationships in the different areas of their lives including peer and social relationships, family relationships and more formal relationships in their jobs, organizations and prosocial groups.

Striving to form strong social bonds of attachment and commitment that lead to development of relevant competencies and skills put young adults on a path to positive development. Regular interaction within these social and community circles provide opportunities for application and expression of skills, which strengthens bonds and help young adults develop their identities and sense of community.

Parenting is an important decision, and therefore is well planned and prepared for. Steps are taken to avoid unplanned pregnancy.

During pregnancy healthy life choices in terms of nutrition, activities and health care is paramount in order to increase the chances of a healthy pregnancy and baby.

Responsible and involved parenting could include being educated about good parenting practices (by reading or attending workshops), attending parenting groups and spending quality time with children.

2.3 ETHICAL RELATIONSHIPS AND CIVIC ENGAGEMENT

Successful young adults live according to a value system that demonstrates respect towards themselves and others. This includes living and behaving morally, peacefully, and with integrity, honesty and reliability towards others and in daily decisions.

Young adults value the improvement of social, political, physical welfare of their communities and society and they behave in a way that increases a sense of community.

They are concerned by ethical issues and facilitate social and global change legally and lawfully. They are politically involved in voting in elections, as well as involved in their communities by volunteering, giving to charities and actions that benefit and contribute to the environment.

3. EDUCATIONAL ATTAINMENT AND CAREER/ JOB OBJECTIVES

Post-secondary educational involvement leads to higher levels of income and career/job success. Post-secondary education can include:

Formal qualifications (degree, certificate, diploma). Formal post-secondary studies have been related to better problem-solving abilities, intuition, creativity and persuasion which lead to the ability to excel at abstract tasks.

Informal learning such as volunteering, practical training and internships, mentoring and self-directed learning via online platforms and reading. This is especially useful for those who are disadvantaged as a result of geographical location, finances or poor quality of schooling.

Other indicators of success for young adults are:

Involvement and constructive engagement in school and college during early life indicate success in later career life and significant roles in career and jobs.

Effort and initiative spent in obtaining educational attainment as well as the duration and intensity of being productively engaged in job/career are indications of success for young adults.

Personal attributes that are indicators of job/careers success include commitment, resilience and adaptability, decisiveness, critical thinking skills, having a positive outlook and being proactive.

Skills that relate to job/career success include entrepreneurial resources that enable youth to create and implement creative solutions that allow them to make frequent changes and manage transitions, as well as the pursuit of continued learning and development of skills.

4. FINANCIAL WELLBEING

SUCCESSFUL YOUNG ADULTS:

Take responsibility for their daily, monthly and long term financial budget and planning.

They live within their means, save monthly and invest wisely. They are therefore on track with financial commitments and are able to withstand unforeseen financial shocks.

Strive to be educated and informed about financial concepts and policies that allow them to manage their financial affairs. This provides a good foundation for transition into adulthood and the related financial demands of entrepreneurship and commerce.

Personal attributes linked with financial success and sustainability includes having a future orientation, self-control, self directed learning of relevant concepts and staying up to date with financial trends.

Limiting credit and avoiding credit options such as in-store cards and building diversified financial portfolios relate to financial wellness.

5. FUN AND LEISURE

Well-being is increased by taking part in fulfilling leisure activities with high levels of satisfaction, engagement, motivation and expression of individual capacities.

Cultivating unique strengths, interests and aptitudes through leisure activities lead to development of a sense of authenticity, internal motivation and enthusiasm.

Fun and leisure activities that lead to the discovery and expression of one's own unique qualities, and that is pursued with dedication and commitment over time in order to obtain a sense of mastery and achievement, is an essential element for well-being and flourishing.

MAJOR PROBLEMS WHICH THREATEN THE SUSTAINABILITY OF PLANET EARTH

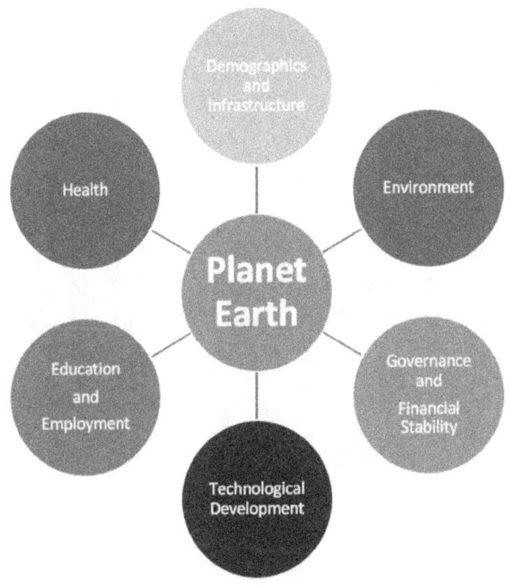

(Adapted from: Halal, 2013)

The following are important factors that threaten the sustainability of Planet Earth:

1. DEMOGRAPHICS AND INFRASTRUCTURE

Rapid global population growth, particularly in developing countries puts pressure on the environment and the infrastructure.

Urban areas will be absorbing future population growth and the subsequent challenges related to urban and infrastructure development.

Significant gaps exist in the current infrastructure needs due to population growth and actual development and maintenance of infrastructure impact economic growth.

Countries with high fertility levels need to prepare for the needs of a growing population of children and young people.

Countries with ageing populations need to adapt public programmes to address needs of the growing proportion of older people.

Gender equality can be achieved by eliminating all forms of violence and discrimination against women in areas of personal safety, fertility and family planning, education, and access to the labour market and political processes.

2. THE ENVIRONMENT

Climate Change – high carbon emissions have an impact on the increase in global temperatures, weather patterns and natural disasters which has affected millions of people in the last 5 years. Burning of fossil fuels also contribute to the destabilization of the climate.

Natural resources – population growth leads to an increased demand for natural resources, in particular water. Climate change and competition from the energy and agricultural sectors could also lead to decline in water availability in cities.

Food production – particular animal-based foods uses over 75% of global agricultural land, and is responsible for about two thirds of production related greenhouse gas emissions. Poor farming practices also take a toll on the environment.

Plant and animal life – human activities, including overfishing and illegal fishing, disrupt the ecosystem, biodiversity and natural habitats of plant and animal life with the result of mass extinction of many species of plant and animals. Loss of millions of hectares of tree cover is increasing.

Pollution – human activity and production pollute the atmosphere, biosphere, lithosphere, geosphere and hydrosphere (air, ground and soil, landforms and water). Pollution from pesticides, chemicals, plastics and other waste affect the soil, plant life, rivers and the sea as well as animals.

Provision of food – there is a significant discrepancy between the billions of people around the world who are poorly nourished and starving and enormous amounts of food that go to waste in other areas of the world.

3. GOVERNANCE AND FINANCIAL STABILITY

Financial and economic inequality keeps the financially disadvantaged in deprivation with regards to limited access to expensive medical services, education and training. This may lead to pressure and hostility towards governments.

Protectionist Policies (taxing or limiting goods from other countries in order to boost own country's trade or industry) vs. Globalization (worldwide movement towards economic, financial, trade and communication integration and interdependence and connection across national frontiers) – the interplay between these two views throughout the world can create global uncertainty and can impact trade agreements, economic activity, production of goods and employment.

Global currencies are volatile and this results in hyperinflation in attempts to stabilize currencies.

Poorly managed monetary policies lead to political unrest and violence, military dictatorship and banking crises including hyperinflation.

Polarization of politics and differing ideologies increases conflict and hostility which puts democracy under pressure. Armed conflicts involving parties within a single country or state, as well as international armed conflicts result in deaths and displacements of millions of people.

Criminal networks and multi-billion-dollar crime syndicates trading in goods, drugs, people, money, intellectual property and resources undermine economic markets and competitiveness of companies, the integrity of governments and the security of communities and countries.

Cybercrime and cyber attacks are on the increase and could disrupt essential services as well as financial and government systems.

4. TECHNOLOGICAL DEVELOPMENT

The Fourth Industrial Evolution – this is the current trend of disruptive technologies such as Internet of Things (IoT), and the development of artificial intelligence and virtual reality. These changes and developments are changing the way we work and live and it has a significant impact on international cooperation and trade as well as economic and financial systems.

5. EDUCATION AND EMPLOYMENT

Across the world millions of children and young people are not attending school or being educated.

Inequality in education is increasing, especially among the poor and disadvantaged. In some countries girls are still less likely than boys to proceed to secondary education.

The current education system is outdated with curricula that have not changed for centuries. Limited focus is placed on equipping students with skills and mindsets needed to adapt in a future of accelerated change and on motivating students to become life-long learners.

As a result of automation and the exponential growth in technology, new industries are continually developing and old ones are becoming obsolete. This is disrupting the entire workforce, and will continue to do so in the future. This has the implication that most of the jobs of the future do not exist yet. The schooling and education system therefore needs to adapt to teaching and training children and youth with the skills base required for future jobs.

6. HEALTH

Non-Communicable Diseases (NCDs) – non-infections and non-transmittable diseases (such as cardiovascular diseases, cancer, diabetes, chronic respiratory diseases, Alzheimer's disease, autoimmune diseases) – cause more than 70% of all annual deaths. These diseases are among the leading causes of preventable illness and related disability. They result in significant financial implications including staggering cumulative losses in output and medical costs.

Infectious diseases (various infections passed from person to person, or transmitted by contaminated food, water or organisms in the environment), malnutrition and birth problems cause numerous deaths in particular in developing countries such as Africa.

Globally, undiagnosed and unaddressed mental health problems could be related to high levels of suicide.

ENDNOTES

1. Pegg, 2019, p.1. describes sparks in the following way: *Sparks can be musical, athletic, intellectual, academic, or relational; from playing the violin to working with kids or senior citizens. Sparks can ignite a lifelong vocation or career, or balance other activities to create an emotionally satisfying, enriched life.*

2. *The study of virtue is not quite the same as the study of morals (right and wrong, good and evil). Aristotle defined the virtues simply as the ways of behaving that are most conducive to happiness in life* (Doidge in Peterson, 2018, p. xx, par 1).

3. In this context, a relational-moral individual refers to a virtuous person–someone with good moral values and healthy relationships (Maree & Twigge, 2015).

REFERENCES

Bandura, A. (1988). Self-regulation of motivation and action through goal systems. In V. Hamilton, G.H. Bower, & N.H. Frijda (Eds.), *Cognitive perspectives on emotion and motivation* (pp. 37–61). Dordrecht: Kluwer Academic Publishers.

Big Think. Jordan Peterson's guide to leadership. Online video clip. *Youtube. Youtube*, 18 December 2018. Web. 16 July 2019.

Buechner, F. (1993). *Wishful Thinking: A Theological ABC*. New York, NY: Harper & Row.

Columba Leadership. TedEx Talks. Making Incredible Change Nkotlana Rosey Seima at TEDxWesterfordHighSchool. Online video clip. *YouTube*. YouTube, 23 June 2016. Web. 16 July 2019.

Dik, B.J., & Duffy, R.D. (2009). Calling and vocation at work: Definitions and prospects for research and practice. *The Counseling Psychologist*, 37, 424-450.

Halal, W. (2013). Through the megacrisis: the passage to global maturity. *Foresight*, 15, 392-404.

Howell, A.J., Keyes, C.L.M., & Passmore, H. (2013). Flourishing among children and adolescents: Structure and correlates of positive mental health, and interventions for its enhancement. In C. Proctor & P. A. Linley (Eds.), *Research, applications and interventions for children and adolescents: A positive psychology perspective* (pp. 59–79). Berlin: Springer.

JRE Clips. Jordan Peterson on Cleaning Your Room - The Joe Rogan Experience. Joe Rogan. Online video clip. YouTube. 22 May 2017. Web. 16 July 2019.

Maree, J. G., & Twigge, A. (2015). Career and self-construction of emerging adults: The value of life designing. *Frontiers in psychology*, 6.

Mindvalley Talks. An alternative model to Success. Vishen Lakihani. Online video clip. YouTube, 14 January 2016. Web. 16 July 2019.

Niemiec, R.M. (2014). *Mindfulness and character strengths: A practical guide to flourishing.* Cambridge, MA: Hogrefe.

Parks, S.D. (2011). *Big questions, worthy dreams. Mentoring emerging adults in their search for meaning, purpose and faith.* San Francisco, SF: Jossey-Bass.

Pegg, M. (2019, April 3). B is for Peter Benson: His work helps people to find their sparks. Retrieved from The Positive Encounter: *https://www.thepositiveencourager.global/peter-benson-and-his-work-on-helping-people-to-find-their-sparks/*

Peterson, C., & Seligman, M.E.P. (2004). *Character strengths and virtues: A handbook and classification.* Washington, DC, US: American Psychological Association; New York, NY, US: Oxford University Press.

Peterson, J.B., Higgins, D.M. & Pihl, R.O. (2019). What is Self Authoring? Retrieved from Self Authoring Suite. Past Authoring, Present Authoring. Future Authoring: *https://www.selfauthoring.com/*

Peterson, J.B. (2018). *12 rules for life: An antidote to chaos.* Toronto, ON: Random House Canada.

Peterson, Jordan. "Clean up your room". Online video clip. *YouTube.* YouTube, 14 May 2017. Web. 10 February 2020. Rashid, T., & Anjum, A. (2005). 340 ways to use VIA character strengths. Unpublished manuscript. Retrieved from *https://www.purposeplus.com/uploads/340-Ways-toUse-Your-Strengths.pdf*

Savickas, M.L. (2006). *Career counselling Series II [DVD]. Specific Treatments for SPECIFIC populations.* Washington, DC: American Psychological Association.

Savickas, M.L. (2011). *Career Counseling.* Washington, DC: American Psychological Association.

Scales, P.C., Benson, P.L., & Roehlkepartain, E.C. (2010). Adolescent thriving: the role of sparks, relationships, and empowerment. *Journal of Youth Adolescence.* 40, 263–277.

Scales, P.C., Benson, P.L., Oesterle, S., Hill, K.G., Hawkins, J.D., & Pashak, T.J. (2016). The dimensions of successful young adult development: A conceptual and measurement framework. *Applied Developmental Science,* 20, 150–174.

Schwartz, K.D., Bukowski, W.M., & Aoki, W.T. (2006). Mentors, friends, and gurus: Peer and nonparent influences on spiritual development. In E.C. Roehlkepartain, P.E. King, L.M. Wagener., & P.L. Benson (Eds.), *The handbook of spiritual development in childhood and adolescence* (pp. 310-323). Thousand Oaks, CA: Sage.

Taylor, C. (1989). *Sources of the Self: The Making of the Modern Identity.* Cambridge, England: Harvard University Press.

Taylor, R. (2016). Why I started Columba Leadership in SA. Retrieved from *https://www.columba.org.za/news-and-events/ why-i-started-columba-leadership-in-sa-rob-taylor*

VIA Institute on Character (2019). Retrieved from *https:// www.viacharacter.org/*

VIAStrenghts. Mayerson, N.H. A Character Strengths Revolution. Online video clip. *YouTube.* YouTube, 1 July 2015. Web. 16 July 2019.

Wong, P.T.P. (2019). Assessing Jordan B. Peterson's Contribution to the Psychology of Wellbeing: A Book Review of 12 Rules for Life. *International Journal of Wellbeing*, 9(1), 83-102. World Population Prospects (2019): Highlights (ST/ESA/SER.A/423).

Zogby, J. (2008). *The Way We'll Be: The Zogby Report on the Transformation of the American Dream.* Random House, New York, NY.

AUTHOR BIO

Adeline Twigge is an educational psychologist who obtained her BSc (Ed) degree at the University of Pretoria in 1981, after which she became a biology teacher at the Afrikaans high school Dr EG Jansen in Boksburg. She completed her BEd (Orthodidactics) degree in 1995 (also at the University of Pretoria) and continued her teaching career at the Afrikaans primary school Concordia. In 1999, she completed her MEd (Educational Psychology) degree at the University of Pretoria and started her career as educational psychologist, first at the Dr WK du Plessis School (Springs) for learners with epilepsy and learning disabilities, and in 2002 at the School of Achievement (Germiston) for children with learning disabilities. She eventually started a private educational psychology practice in Boksburg in 2005.

Adeline has served on the Gauteng Welfare Services Advisory Committee (a non-profit organization that caters for individuals in urgent need of welfare and psychological services) since 2008. She completed her PhD (Educational Psychology) in 2015. Her research has been published (together with her promotor and co-author Professor Kobus Maree) in the distinguished *Frontiers in Psychology,* which is ranked as the 5th most-cited publisher among the twenty largest publishers in its field. Their article was also published in a Frontiers eBook as part of the Research Topic titled *From Meaning of Working to Meaningful Lives: The Challenges of Expanding Decent Work.*